QUAINT IRISH CUSTOMS
AND SUPERSTITIONS

Quaint Irish Customs and Superstitions

LADY WILDE

THE MERCIER PRESS
CORK

The Mercier Press Limited
Cork

British Library Cataloguing in Publication Data

Wilde, Lady, *d. 1896*
Quaint Irish customs and superstitions.
1. Irish customs
I. Title
390'.09415

ISBN 978-1-78117-942-0

These customs and superstitions were originally published as part of *Ancient Legends, Mystic Charms and Superstitions of Ireland*.

Transferred to Digital Print-on-Demand in 2024

Contents

1 Fairies

The *Sidhe*, or spirit race, called also the *Feadh-Ree*, or fairies, are supposed to have been once angels in heaven, who were cast out by Divine command as a punishment for their inordinate pride.

Some fell to earth and lived there, long before man was created, as the first gods of the earth. Others fell into the sea and they built themselves beautiful fairy palaces of crystal and pearl underneath the waves. On moonlight nights they often come up on to the land, riding their white horses, and they hold parties with their fairy kindred of the earth, who live in the clefts of the hills. They dance together under the ancient trees, and drink nectar from the cups of the flowers which is the fairy wine.

Other fairies, however, are demoniacal and given to evil and malicious deeds. When they were cast out of heaven they fell into hell, and there the devil holds them under his rule and sends them forth as he wills upon missions of evil to tempt the souls of men by the false glitter of sin and pleasure. These spirits live under the earth and give their knowledge only to certain evil persons chosen by the devil and he gives them power to make incantations and brew love potions to work wicked spells. They can assume different forms by their knowledge and use of certain magical herbs.

The witch women who have been taught by them, and have become tools of the Evil One, are the terror of the neighbourhood. They have all the power of the fairies and all the malice of the devil who reveals to them secrets of times and days and secrets of herbs and evil spells; and by the power of magic they can effect all their purposes, whether for good or ill.

The fairies of the earth are small and beautiful. They passionately love music and dancing, and live luxuriously in their palaces under the hills and in the deep mountain caves; and they can obtain all things lovely for their fairy homes, merely by the strength of their magic power. They can also assume all forms, and will never know death until the last day comes when their fate is to vanish away – to be annihilated for ever. But they are very jealous of the human race who are so tall and strong, and to whom immortality has been promised.

They are often tempted by the beauty of a mortal woman and greatly desire to have her as a wife. The children of such marriages have a strange mystic nature and generally become famous in music and song. But they are passionate, revengeful and not easy to live with. Every one knows them to be of the Sidhe or spirit race by their beautiful eyes and their bold, reckless temperament.

The fairy king and princes dress in green, with red caps bound on the head with a golden fillet. The fairy queen and the great court ladies are robed in glittering silver gauze, spangled with diamonds and their long golden hair sweeps the ground as they dance. Their favourite camp and resting-place is under a hawthorn tree, and a peasant would die sooner than cut down one of the ancient hawthorns, sacred to the fairies, which generally stands in the centre of a fairy ring.

But the people never offer worship to these fairy beings, for they look on the Sidhe as a race quite inferior to man. At the same time they have an immense dread and fear of the mystic fairy power and never interfere with them or offend them knowingly.

The Sidhe often strive to carry off handsome children who are then reared in the beautiful fairy palaces under the earth and wedded to fairy mates when they grow up. The people dread the idea of a fairy changeling being left in the cradle in place of their own lovely child. If a wizened little thing is found there, it is sometimes taken out at night and left in an open grave till morning, when they hope to find their own child restored, although more often nothing is found except the cold corpse of the poor outcast.

Sometimes it is said the fairies carry off the mortal child for a sacrifice as they have to offer one every seven years to the devil in return for the power he gives them. Beautiful young girls are carried off, also, either for sacrifice or to be married to the fairy king.

The fairies are pure and cleanly in their habits, and they like above all things a pail of water to be set out for them at night, in case they may wish to bathe.

They also delight in good wines and are careful to repay the donor in blessings for they are truly upright and honest. The great lords of Ireland, in ancient times, used to leave a keg of the finest Spanish wine frequently at night out on the window-sill for the fairies and in the morning it was all gone.

Fire is a great preventative against fairy magic, for fire is the most sacred of all created things and man alone has power over it. No animal has ever yet attained the knowledge of how to draw out the spirit of fire from the stone or the wood where it has found a dwelling-place. If a ring of fire is made around cattle or a child's cradle, or if fire is placed under the churn, the fairies have no power to harm. And the spirit of the fire is certain to destroy all fairy magic, if it exists.

(ii) FAIRY NATURE

The *Siodh-Dune*, or the Mount of Peace, is also a favourite resort of the fairies. It is an ancient, sacred place, where the Druids in old time used to go to pray when they desired solitude. The fairies meet there every seven years to perform the act of lamentation and mourning for having been cast out of heaven.

Earth, lake and hill are peopled by these fantastic, beautiful gods of earth; the wilful, capricious child-spirits of the world. The Irish seem to have created this strange fairy race after their own image for in all things they strangely resemble the Irish character.

The Sidhe passionately love beauty and luxury and hold in contempt all the mean virtues of thrift and economy. Above all things they hate the close, niggard hand that gathers the last grain, drains the last drop in the milk-pail and plucks the trees bare of fruit, leaving nothing for the spirits who wander by in the moonlight. They like food and wine to be left for them at night, yet they are very temperate – no one ever saw an intoxicated fairy.

But people should not sit up too late for the fairies like to gather round the smouldering embers after the family are in bed, and drain the wine-cup, and drink the milk which a good housewife always leaves for them, in case the fairies should come in and want their supper. A vessel of pure water should also be left for them to bathe in, if they like.

In all things the fairies are fond of being made much of and flattered and attended to – and the fairy blessing will come back in return to the giver for whatever act of kindness he has done to the spirits of the hill and the cave. Some unexpected good fortune or stroke of luck will come upon his house or his children for the fairy race is not ungrateful and is powerful over man both for good and evil. Therefore be kind to the wayfarer for he may be a fairy prince in disguise who has come to test the depth of your charity and generous nature that can give liberally out of pure love and kindliness to those who are in need, and not in hope of a reward.

If treated well, the fairies will discover the hidden pot of gold, and reveal the mysteries of herbs, and give knowledge to the fairy women of the mystic spells that can cure disease, and save life and make the lover loved.

All they ask in return is to be left in quiet possession of the rath and the hill and the ancient hawthorn trees that have been theirs from time immemorial, where they lead a joyous life with music and dance, and charming little suppers of the nectar of flowers, down in the crystal caves, lit by diamonds that stud the rocks.

But some small courtesies they require. Never drain your wine-glass at a feast, nor the poteen flask, nor the milk-pail; and never rake out all the fire at night, it looks mean, and the fairies like a little of everything going, and to have the hearth comfortable and warm when they come in to hold a council after all the mortal people have gone to bed. In fact, the fairies are born aristocrats, true ladies and gentlemen, and if treated with proper respect are never in the least malignant or ill-natured.

When a woman first takes ill in her confinement, unlock instantly every press and drawer in the house, but when the child is born, lock them all up again at once for if care is not taken the fairies will get in and hide in the drawers and presses, to be ready to steal away the little mortal baby when they get the opportunity, and place some ugly, wizened changeling in the cradle beside the poor mother. Therefore every key should be turned, every lock made fast, and if the fairies are hidden inside, let them stay there until all danger is over for the baby by the proper precautions being taken, such as a red coal set under the cradle, and a branch of mountain ash tied over it, or of the alder-tree, according to the sex of the child, for both trees have mystic virtues, probably because of the ancient superstition that the first man was created from an alder-tree and the first woman from the mountain ash.

The fairies, however, are sometimes successful in carrying off a baby and the mother finds in the morning a poor weakly little sprite in the cradle in place of her own splendid child. But should the mortal infant happen to grow up ugly, the fairies send it back for they love beauty above all things; and the fairy chiefs greatly desire a handsome mortal wife, so that a handsome girl must be well guarded or they will carry her off. The children of such unions grow up beautiful and clever, but are also wild, reckless and extravagant. They are known at once by the beauty of their eyes and hair. They have a magic fascination that no one can resist and also a fairy gift of music and song.

When children are pining away, they are supposed to be fairy-struck; and the juice of twelve leaves of foxglove may be given: also in cases of fever the same.

Unbaptised children are readily seized by the fairies. The best preventive is a little salt tied up in the child's dress when it is laid to sleep in the cradle.

People born in the morning cannot see spirits or the fairy world; but those born at night have power over ghosts and can see the spirits of the dead.

People ought to remember that egg-shells are favourite retreats of the fairies, therefore the judicious eater should always break the shell after use, to prevent the fairy sprite from taking up his lodgment therein.

(iii) THE FAIRY RATH

The ancient rath, or fort, or liss, generally enclosed about half an acre and had two or more ramparts, formed by the heads of the tribe for defence. But when the race of the chieftains died out then the Sidhe crowded into the forts and there held their councils and revels and dances. If a man put his ear close to the ground at night he could hear the sweet fairy music rising up from under the earth.

The rath is sacred to the fairies and no mortal is allowed to cut down a tree that grows on it or to carry away a stone. But dangerous above all would it be to build on a fairy rath. If a man attempted such a rash act, the fairies would put a blast on his eyes, or give him a crooked mouth; for no human hand should dare to touch their ancient dancing grounds.

It is not right, the people say, to sing or whistle at night that old air, 'The pretty girl milking her cow' for it is a fairy tune and the fairies will not suffer a mortal to sing their music while they are dancing on the grass. But if a person sleeps on the rath the music will enter into his soul, and when he awakes he may sing the air he has heard in his dreams. In this way the bards learned their songs and they were skilled musicians, and touched the harp with a master hand, so

that the fairies often gathered round to listen, though
invisible to mortal eyes.

2 May Day

May Day, called in Irish *Lá-Beltaine*, the day of the Baal fires, was the festival of greatest rejoicing held in Ireland. But the fairies have great power at that season and children and cattle, the milk and butter, must be well guarded from their influence. A spent coal must be put under the churn and another under the cradle and primroses must be scattered before the door for the fairies cannot pass the flowers. Children that die in April are supposed to be carried off by the fairies, who are then always on the watch to abduct whatever is young and beautiful for their fairy homes.

Sometimes on 1 May, a sacred heifer, snow white, appeared amongst the cattle and this was considered to bring the highest good luck to the farmer. An old Irish song that alludes to the heifer may be translated thus:

> There is a cow on the mountain,
> A fair white cow;
> She goes east and she goes west,
> And my senses have gone for love of her:
> She goes with the sun and he forgets to burn,
> And the moon turns her face with love to her,
> My fair white cow of the mountain.

The fairies are in the best of humours upon May Eve and the music of the fairy pipes may be heard all through the night, while the fairy folk are dancing upon the rath. It is then they carry off the young people to join their revels and if a girl has once danced to the fairy music she will move ever after with such fascinating grace that it has passed into a proverb to say of a good dancer, 'She has danced to fairy music on the hill'.

At the great long dance held in old times on May day all the people held hands and danced round a great May-bush erected on a mound. The circle sometimes extended for a mile, the girls wearing garlands and the young men carrying wands of green boughs, while the elder people sat round on the grass as spectators and applauded the ceremony. The tallest and strongest young men in the county stood in the centre and directed the movements, while the pipers and harpers, wearing green and gold sashes, played the most spirited dance tunes.

The oldest worship of the world was of the sun and moon, of trees, wells and the serpent that gave wisdom. Trees were the symbol of knowledge and the dance round the May-bush is part of the ancient ritual. . . This reverence for the tree is one of the oldest superstitions of humanity and the most universal, and the fires are a relic of the old pagan worship paid to the Grynian Apollo – fire above all things being held sacred by the Irish as a safeguard from evil spirits. It is a saying amongst them, 'Fire and salt are the two most sacred things given to man, and if you give them away on May Day, you give away your luck for the year.' Therefore no one will allow milk, or fire, or salt to be carried away from the house on that day and if people came in and asked for a lighted sod they would be driven away with curses for their purpose was evil.

The witches, however, make great efforts to steal the milk on May morning, and if they succeed, the luck passes from the family and the milk and butter for the whole year will belong to the fairies. The best preventative is to scatter primroses on the threshold and the old women tie bunches of primroses to the cows' tails, for the evil spirits cannot touch anything guarded by these flowers, but only if they are plucked before sunrise. A piece of iron, also, made red hot is placed upon the hearth; any old iron will do, the older the better. Branches of whitethorn and mountain ash are wreathed round the doorway for luck. The mountain ash has very great and mysterious qualities. If a branch of it be woven into the roof that house is safe from fire for a year at least, and if a branch of it is mixed with the timber of a boat no storm will upset it and no man in it will be drowned for twelve months.

To save milk from witchcraft, the people on May morning cut and peel some branches of the mountain ash and bind the twigs round the milk pails and the churn. No witch or fairy will then be able to steal the milk or butter. But all this must be done *before sunrise*. However, should butter be missed, follow the cow to the field and gather the clay her hoof has touched then, on returning home, place it under the churn with a live coal and a handful of salt and your butter is safe from man or woman, fairy or fiend, for that year. There are other methods also to preserve a good supply of butter in the churn; a horse-shoe tied on it; a rusty nail from a coffin driven into the side; a cross made of the leaves of veronica placed at the bottom of the milk pail; but the mountain ash is the best of all safeguards against witchcraft and the devil's magic. Without some of these precautions the fairies will certainly not overlook the churn and the butter, in consequence, will fail all through the year and the farmer suffer great loss.

Herbs gathered on May Eve have a mystical and strong virtue for curing disease and powerful potions are made then by the skilful herb women and fairy doctors which no sickness can resist – chiefly the yarrow, called in Irish 'the herb of seven needs' from its many great virtues. Divination is also practised to a great extent by means of the yarrow. The girls dance round it singing:

Yarrow, yarrow, yarrow,
I bid thee good morrow,
And tell me before tomorrow
Who my true love shall be.

The herb is then placed under the head at night and in dreams the true lover will appear. Another mode of divination for the future fate in life is by snails. The young girls go out early before sunrise to trace the path of the snails in the clay, for always a letter is marked, and this is the initial of the true lover's name.

A black snail is very unlucky to meet first in the morning, for his trail would read *death*; but a white snail brings good fortune.

A white lamb on the right hand is also good; but the cuckoo is an omen of evil. Of old the year began with 1 May, and an ancient Irish rhyme says:

A white lamb on my right side,
So will good come to me;
But not the little false cuckoo
On the first day of the year.

Prophecies were also made from the way the wind blew on May mornings. In 1798 an old man, who was drawing near to his end and about to die, inquired from those around him:

'Where did you leave the wind last night?' (May Eve.)

They told him it came from the north.

'Then,' he said, 'the country is lost to the Clan Gael, our enemies will triumph. Had it been from the south, we should have had the victory, but now the Sassenach will trample us to dust.' And he fell back and died.

Ashes are often sprinkled on the threshold on May Eve, and if the print of a foot is found in the morning, turned inward, it signals marriage; but if turned outward, death.

On May Eve the fairy music is heard on all the hills, and many beautiful tunes have been caught up in this way by the people and the native musicians.

About a hundred years ago a celebrated tune, called *Moraleana,* was learnt by a piper as he traversed the hills one evening; and he played it perfectly, note by note, as he heard it from the fairy pipes. A voice spoke to him and said that he would be allowed to play the tune *three times* in his life before all the people, but never a fourth, or a doom would fall on him. However, one day he had a great contest for supremacy with another piper, and at last, to make sure of victory, he played the wonderful fairy melody when all the people applauded and declared he had won the prize by reason of its beauty, and that no music could equal his. So they crowned him with the garland, but at that moment he turned deadly pale, the pipes dropped from his hand, and he fell lifeless to the ground. For nothing escapes the fairies, they know all things and their vengeance is swift and sure.

It is very dangerous to sleep out in the open air in the month of May, for the fairies are very powerful then, and on the watch to carry off the handsome girls for fairy brides, and the young mothers as nurses for the fairy babies; while the young men are selected as husbands for the beautiful fairy princesses.

A young man died suddenly on May Eve while he was lying asleep under a hay-rick and his parents and friends knew immediately that he had been carried off to the fairy palace in the great moat of Granard. So a renowned fairy man was sent for, who promised to have him back in nine days. Meanwhile he desired that food and drink of the best should be left daily for the young man at a certain place on the moat. This was done, and the food always disappeared, by which they knew the young man was living, and came out of the moat nightly for the provisions left for him by his people.

Now on the ninth day a great crowd assembled to see the young man brought back from Fairyland. And in the middle stood the fairy doctor performing his incantations by means of fire and a powder which he threw into the flames that caused a dense grey smoke to arise. Then, taking off his hat, and holding a key in his hand, he called out three times in a loud voice, 'Come forth, come forth, come forth!'

A shrouded figure slowly rose up in the midst of the smoke and a voice was heard answering, 'Leave me in peace; I am happy with my fairy bride, and my parents need not weep for me for I shall bring them good luck and guard them from evil evermore.'

Then the figure vanished and the smoke cleared, and the parents were content, for they believed the vision, and having loaded the fairy-man with presents they sent him away home.

The marsh marigold is considered of great use in divination and is called 'the shrub of Beltaine'. Garlands are made of it for the cattle and the door-posts to keep off the fairy power. Milk also is poured on the threshold, though none would be given away; nor fire, nor salt – these three things being sacred. There are many superstitions concerning May-time.

It is not safe to go on the water the first Monday in May.

Hares found on May morning are supposed to be witches and should be stoned.

If the fire goes out on May morning it is considered

very unlucky and it cannot be re-kindled except by a lighted sod brought from the priest's house. The ashes of this blessed turf are afterwards sprinkled on the floor and the threshold of the house. Neither fire, nor water, nor milk, nor salt should be given away for love or money, and if a wayfarer is given a cup of milk he must drink it in the house and salt must be mixed with it. Salt and water as a drink is at all times considered a potent charm against evil, if properly prepared by a fairy doctor and the magic words said over it.

One day in May a young girl lay down to rest at noontide on a fairy rath and fell asleep – a thing of great danger, for the fairies are strong in power during the May month, and are particularly on the watch for a mortal bride to carry away to the fairy mansions, for they love the sight of human beauty. So they spirited away the young sleeping girl and only left a shadowy resemblance of her lying on the rath. Evening came on and as the young girl had not returned her mother sent out messengers in all directions to look for her. At last she was found on the fairy rath, lying quite unconscious, like one dead.

They carried her home and laid her on her bed but she neither spoke nor moved. So three days passed over. Then they thought it right to send for the fairy doctor. At once he said that she was fairy struck and he gave them a salve made of herbs to anoint her hands and her brow every morning at sunrise and every night when the moon rose; and salt was sprinkled on the threshold and round her bed where she lay sleeping. This was done for six days and six nights and then the girl rose up suddenly and asked for food. They gave her something to eat, but asked no questions, only watched her so that she should not leave the house. And then she fixed her eyes on them steadily and said:

'Why did you bring me back? I was so happy. I was in a beautiful palace where lovely ladies and young princes were dancing to the sweetest music. They made me dance with them and threw a mantle over me of rich gold: and now it is all gone, and you have brought me back, and I shall never, never see the beautiful palace again.'

Then the mother wept and said: 'Oh, child, stay with me, for I have no other daughter, and if the fairies take you from me I shall die.'

When the girl heard this, she fell on her mother's neck and kissed her, and promised that she would never again go near the fairy rath while she lived for the fairy doctor told her that if ever she lay down there again and slept she would never return alive to her home.

3 Whitsuntide

Whitsuntide is a very fatal and unlucky time.

Especially beware of water then, for there is an evil spirit in it, and no one should venture to bathe, nor to sail in a boat for fear of being drowned, nor to go on a journey where water has to be crossed.

Everything in the house must be sprinkled with holy water at Whitsuntide to keep away the fairies, who at that season are very active and malicious, and bewitch the cattle, carry off the young children, come up from the sea to hold strange midnight revels, when they kill with their fairy darts the unhappy mortal who crosses their path and pries at their mysteries.

Whitsuntide is a most unlucky time, horses foaled then will grow up dangerous and kill some one.

Beware also of water at Whitsuntide, for an evil power is on the waves and the lakes and the rivers, and a boat may be swamped and men drowned unless a bride steers – then the danger ceases.

A child born at Whitsuntide will have an evil temper, and may commit a murder.

To turn away ill-luck from a child born at that time, a grave must be dug and the infant laid in it for a few minutes. After this process the evil spell is broken, and the child is safe.

If any one takes ill at Whitsuntide there is great danger of death, for the evil spirits are on the watch to carry off victims, and no sick person should be left alone at this time, nor in the dark. Light is a great safeguard, as well as fire, against malific influences.

In old times at Whitsuntide blood was poured out as an offering to the evil spirits; and the children and cattle were passed through two lines of fire.

4 Midsummer

This season is still made memorable in Ireland by lighting fires on every hill, according to the ancient pagan usage, when the Baal fires were kindled as part of the ritual of sun-worship, though now they are lit in honour of St John. The great bonfire of the year is still made on St John's Eve, when all the people dance round it and every young man takes a lighted stick from the pile to bring home with him for good luck to the house.

In ancient times the sacred fire was lit with great ceremony on Midsummer Eve. On that night all the people of the adjacent country watched the western promontory of Howth, and the moment the first flash was seen from that spot wild cries and cheers were repeated from village to village when all the local fires began to blaze and Ireland was circled by a cordon of flame rising up from every hill. Then the dance and song began round every fire and the wild hurrahs filled the air with the most frantic revelry.

Many of these ancient customs are still continued, and the fires are still lit on St John's Eve on every hill in Ireland. When the fire has burned down to a red glow the young men strip to the waist and leap over or through the flames. This is done backwards and forwards several times and he who braves the greatest blaze is considered the victor over the powers of evil and is greeted with tremendous applause. When the fire burns still lower, the young girls leap the flame and those who leap clean over three times back and forward will be certain of a speedy marriage and good luck in after life with many children. The married women then walk through the lines of the burning embers; and when the fire is nearly burnt and trampled down, the yearling cattle are driven through the hot ashes and their back is singed with a lighted hazel twig. These hazel rods are kept safely afterwards being considered of immense power to drive the cattle to and from the watering places. As the fire diminishes the shouting grows fainter, the song and dance commence, while professional storytellers narrate tales of fairyland, or of the good old times long ago when the kings and princes of Ireland lived amongst their own people and there was food to eat and wine to drink for all comers to the feast at the king's house. When the crowd at length separate, every one carries home a stick from the fire and great virtue is attached to the lighted *brone* which is safely carried to the house without breaking or falling to the ground. Many contests also arise amongst the young men; for whoever enters his house first with the sacred fire brings the good luck of the year with him.

On the first Sunday in Midsummer all the young people used to stand in lines having left the church to be hired for service – the girls holding white hands, the young men each with an emblem of his trade. The evening ended with a dance and the revelry was kept up until the dawn of the next day, called 'Sorrowful Monday,' because of the end of the pleasure and the frolic.

5 November Spells

The ancient Irish divided the year into summer and winter – *Samhradh* and *Geimhreadh*; the former beginning in May, the latter in November, called also *Samfuim* (summer end). At this season, when the sun dies, the powers of darkness exercise great and evil influence over all things. The witch-women say they can then ride at night through the air with Diana of the Ephesians and Herodias, and others in league with the devil, change men to beasts, and ride with the dead and cover leagues of ground on swift spirit-horses.

Also on November Eve, by certain incantations, the dead can be made to appear and answer questions; but for this purpose blood must be sprinkled on the dead body when it rises, for it is said the spirits love blood. The colour excites them and gives them for the time the power and the semblance of life.

All the spells worked on November Eve are performed in the name of the devil who is then forced to reveal the future fate of the questioner. The most usual spell is to wash a garment in a running brook, then hang it on a thorn bush, and wait to see the apparition of the lover who will come to turn it. But the tricks played on this night by young persons on each other have often most disastrous consequences. One young girl fell dead with fright when an apparition really came and turned the garment she had hung on the bush. And a lady narrates that on the 1

QUAINT IRISH CUSTOMS AND SUPERSTITIONS

November her servant rushed into the room and fainted on the floor. On recovering, she said that she had played a trick that night in the name of the devil before the looking-glass; but what she had seen she dared not speak of, though the thought of it would never leave her brain and she knew the shock would kill her. They tried to laugh her out of her fears, but the next night she was found quite dead with her features horribly contorted, lying on the floor before the looking-glass, which was shivered to pieces.

Another spell is the building of the house. Twelve couples are taken, each being made of two holly twigs tied together with a hempen thread; these are all named and stuck round in a circle in the clay. A live coal is then placed in the centre and whichever couple catches fire first will assuredly be married. Then the future husband is invoked in the name of the Evil One to appear and quench the flame.

On one occasion a 'dead man in his shroud answered the call and silently drew away the girl from the rest of the party. The fright turned her brain, and she never recovered her reason afterwards. The horror of that apparition haunted her for ever, especially as on November Eve it is believed firmly that the dead really leave their graves and have power to appear amongst the living.

A young girl in a farmer's service was in the loft one night looking for eggs when two men came into the stable underneath and through a chink in the boards

30

she could see them quite well and hear all they said. To her horror she found that they were planning the murder of a man in the neighbourhood who was suspected of being an informer and they settled how they would get rid of the body by throwing it into the Shannon. She crept home half dead with fright, but did not tell any one what she had heard. Next day, however, the news spread that the man was missing, and it was feared he was murdered. Still the girl was afraid to reveal what she knew though the ghost of the murdered man seemed for ever before her. Finally she went to another village some miles off and took service. But on November Eve, as she was washing clothes in the Shannon the dead body of the murdered man arose from the water and floated towards her, until it lay quite close to her feet. Then she knew the hand of God was in it and that the spirit of the dead would not rest till he was avenged. So she went and gave information and on her evidence the two murderers were convicted and executed.

If the cattle fall sick at this season, it is supposed that some old fairy man or woman is lying hidden about the place to spy out the doings of the family and work some evil spells.

A farmer had a splendid cow, the pride of his farm, but suddenly it seemed ailing and gave no milk, though every morning it went and stood quite patiently under an old hawthorn tree as if some one were milking her. So the man watched the time, and presently the cow came of herself and stood under the hawthorn, when a little old wizened woman came forth from the trunk of the tree, milked the cow and then retreated into the tree again. On this the farmer sent at once for a fairy doctor, who exorcised the cow and gave it a strong potion after which the spell was broken and the cow was restored to its usual good condition and gave the milk as before.

The fairies also exercise a malign influence by making a path through a house, when all the children begin to pine and a blight falls on the family.

A farmer who had lost one son by heart disease (always a mysterious malady to the peasants) and another by gradual decay, consulted a wise fairy woman as to what should be done, for his wife also had become delicate and weak. The woman told him that on November Eve the fairies had made a road through the house, and were going back and forward ever since, and whatever they looked upon was doomed. The only remedy was to build up the old door and open another entrance. This the man did, and when the witch-women came as usual in the morning to beg for water or milk or meal they found no door and were obliged to turn back. After this the spell was taken off the household and they all prospered without fear of the fairies.

Food should be left out on November Eve for the dead who are then wandering about. If the food disappears, it is a sign that the spirits have taken it for no mortal would dare to touch or eat of the food so left.

Never turn your head to look if you fancy you hear footsteps behind you on that night; for the dead are walking then and their glance would kill.

In November a distaff is placed under the head of a young man at night to make him dream of the girl he is destined to marry.

6 The Dead

There are many strange superstitions concerning the dead. The people seem to believe in their actual presence, though unseen, and to have a great fear and dread of their fatal and mysterious power.

If a person of doubtful character dies, too bad for heaven, too good for hell, they imagine that his soul is sent back to earth and obliged to obey the order of some person who bids him remain in a particular place until the Day of Judgement, or until another soul is found willing to meet him there, and then they may both pass into heaven together, absolved.

An incident is related that happened in the County Galway concerning this superstition.

A gentleman of rank and fortune, but of a free and dissipated life became the lover of a pretty girl, one of the tenant's daughters. And the girl was so devoted to him that perhaps he might have married her at last; but he was killed suddenly, when out hunting, by a fall from his horse.

Some time after, the girl, coming home late one evening, met the ghost of her lover at a very lonesome part of the road. The form was the same as when living, but it had no eyes. The girl crossed herself, on which the ghost disappeared.

Again she met the same apparition at night, and a third time, when the ghost stood right before her in the path so that she could not pass. Then she spoke, and asked in the name of God and the good angels,

QUAINT IRISH CUSTOMS AND SUPERSTITIONS

why he appeared to her; and he answered that he could not rest in his grave till he had received some command from her which he was bound to obey.

'Then,' she said, 'go stand by the gate of heaven till the Judgement Day and look in at the blessed dead on their thrones, but you may not enter. This is my judgement on your soul.'

On this the ghost sighed deeply and vanished and was seen no more. But the girl prayed earnestly that she soon might meet her lover at the gate of heaven, whither she had sent him, so that both might enter together into the blessed land. And thus it happened; for by that day year she was carried to her grave in the churchyard, but her soul went forth to meet her lover, where he waited for her by the gate of heaven. Through her love he was absolved and permitted to enter within the gate before the Judgement Day.

It was considered disrespectful to the dead to take a short cut when carrying the coffin to the grave.

In the Islands, when a person is dying, they place twelve lighted rushes round the bed. This, they say, is to prevent the devil coming for the soul; for nothing evil can pass a circle of fire. They also forbid crying for the dead until three hours have passed by, lest the wail of the mourners should waken the dogs who are waiting to devour the souls of men before they can reach the throne of God.

It is a very general custom during some nights after a death to leave food outside the house – a griddle cake or a dish of potatoes. If it is gone in the morning the spirits must have taken it; for no human being would touch the food left for the dead.

The great and old families of Ireland consider it right to be buried with their kindred and are brought from any distance, however remote, to be laid in the ancient graveyard of the race.

A young man died far away, from fever, and so it was thought advisable not to bring him home but to bury him where he died. However, on the night of the funeral a phantom hearse with four black horses stopped at the churchyard. Some men then entered with spades and shovels and dug a grave after which the hearse drove away. But next morning no sign of the grave was to be found, except a long line marked out, the length of a man's coffin.

It is unlucky and a bad omen to carry fire out of a house where any one is ill. A gentleman one day stopped at a cabin to get a light for his cigar, and having said good morning in the usual friendly fashion, he took a stick from the fire; blew it into a blaze, and was walking away when the woman of the house rose up fiercely and told him it was an evil thing to take fire away when her husband was dying. On looking round he saw a wretched skeleton lying on a bed of straw so he flung back the stick at once and fled from the place, leaving his blessing in the form of a silver offering, to neutralise the evil of the abducted fire.

After the priest has left a dying person and confession has been made all the family kneel round the bed reciting the Litany for the Dying, and holy water is sprinkled over the room until the soul departs.

Then they all rise and begin the mournful death-wail in a loud voice and by this cry all the people in the village know the exact moment of death. Each one that hears it utters a prayer for the departing soul.

At the wake the corpse is often dressed in the habit of a religious order. A cross is placed in the hands and the scapular on the breast. Candles are lighted all round in a circle and the friends and relatives arrange themselves in due order, the nearest of kin being at the head. At intervals they all stand up and intone the death-wail, rocking back and forward over the dead, and reciting his virtues. The widow and orphans frequently salute the corpse with endearing epithets and recall the happy days they spent together.

When the coffin is borne to the grave each person present helps to carry it a little way for this is considered a mode of showing honour to the dead. The nearest relatives take the front handles first; then after a little while they move to the back and others take their place, until every person in turn has borne the head of the coffin to the grave – for it would be dishonourable to the dead to omit this mark of respect.

As the coffin is lowered into the grave the death-cry rises up with a loud and bitter wail, and the excitement often becomes so great that women have fallen into hysterics; and at one funeral a young girl in her agony of grief jumped into her father's grave and was taken up insensible.

It is a custom in the West, when a corpse is carried to the grave, for the bearers to stop half way, while the nearest relatives build up a small monument of loose stones, and no hand would ever dare to touch or disturb this monument while the world lasts.

When the grave is dug, a cross is made of two spades, and the coffin is carried round it three times before being placed in the clay. Then the prayers for the dead are said, all the people kneeling with uncovered heads.

It is ill luck when going with a funeral to meet a man on a white horse. No matter how high the rank of the rider may be, the people must seize the reins and force him to turn back and join the procession at least for a few yards.

When a death was expected it was usual to have a good deal of bread already baked in the house in order that the evil spirits might be employed eating it, and so let the soul of the dying depart in peace. Twelve candles stuck in clay should also be placed round the dying.

If two funerals meet at the same churchyard, the last corpse that enters will have to supply the dead with water till the next corpse arrives.

Never take a child in your arms after being at a wake

where a corpse was laid out unless you first dip your hands in holy water.

The moment the soul leaves the body the evil spirits try to seize it, but the guardian angel fights against them, and those around must pray earnestly that the angel may conquer. After death the body must not be disturbed, nor should the funeral chant be raised for one hour.

If a corpse falls to the ground the most fatal events will happen to the family.

The lid must not be nailed on the coffin of a new-born child, or the mother that bore it will never have another.

The hand of a dead man was a powerful incantation, but it was chiefly used by women. The most eminent fairy women always collected the mystic herbs for charms and cures by the light of a candle held by a dead man's hand at midnight or by the full moon.

The corner of a sheet that has wrapped a corpse is a cure for headache if tied round the head.

The ends of candles used at wakes are of great efficacy in curing burns.

A piece of linen wrap taken from a corpse will cure the swelling of a limb if tied round the part affected.

If any one stumbles at a grave it is a bad omen; but if he falls and touches the clay he will assuredly died before the year is out.

Any one meeting a funeral must turn back and walk at least four steps with the mourners.

If the nearest relative touches the hand of a corpse it will utter a wild cry if not quite dead.

On Twelfth Night, the dead walk, and on every tile of the house a soul is sitting waiting for your prayers to take it out of purgatory.

It is believed that the spirit of the dead last buried has to watch in the churchyard until another corpse is laid there; or has to perform menial offices in the spirit world, such as carrying wood and water until the next spirit comes from earth. They are also sent on messages to earth, chiefly to announce the coming death of some relative, and at this they are glad, for then their time of peace and rest will come at last.

7 The Clearing from Guilt

To prove innocence of a crime a certain ancient form is gone through which the people look on with great awe and call it emphatically – 'The Clearing'. It is a fearful ordeal and instances are known of men who have died of fear and trembling from having passed through the terrors of the trial, even if innocent. And it is equally terrible for the accuser as well as the accused.

On a certain day fixed for the ordeal the accused goes to the churchyard and carries away a skull. Then, wrapped in a white sheet and bearing the skull in his hand, he proceeds to the house of the accuser where a great crowd has assembled for the news of 'A Clearing' spreads like wildfire and all the people gather together as witnesses of the ceremony. There, before the house of his accuser, he kneels down on his bare knees, makes the sign of the cross on his face, kisses the skull and prays for some time in silence. The people also wait in silence, filled with awe and dread, not knowing what the result may be. Then the accuser, pale and trembling, comes forward and stands beside the kneeling man and with uplifted hand swears him to speak the truth. On which the accused, still kneeling and holding the skull in his hand, utters the most fearful imprecation known in the Irish language; almost as terrible as that curse of the Druids, which is so awful that it never yet was put into English words. The accused prays that if he fails to speak the truth all the sins of the man whose skull he holds may be laid upon his soul, and all the sins of his forefathers back to Adam, and all the punishment due to them for the evil of their lives, and all their weakness and sorrow both of body and soul be laid on him both in this life and in the life to come for evermore. But if the accuser has accused falsely and out of malice then may all the evil rest on his head through this life for ever and may his soul perish everlastingly.

It would be impossible to describe adequately the awe with which the assembled people listen to these terrible words and the dreadful silence of the crowd as they wait to see the result. If nothing happens the man rises from his knees after an interval and is pronounced innocent by the judgement of the people and no word is ever again uttered against him, nor is he shunned or slighted by the neighbours. But the accuser is looked on with fear and dislike, he is considered unlucky and seeing that his life is often made so miserable by the coldness and suspicion of the people, many would suffer wrong than force the accused person to undergo so terrible a trial as 'The Clearing'.

8 Animals

In all countries superstitions of good or evil are attached to certain birds. The raven, for instance, has a wide-world reputation as the harbinger of evil and ill-luck. The wild geese foretell a severe winter; the robin is held sacred for no one would think of harming a bird who bears on his breast the blessed mark of the blood of Christ; while the wren is hunted to death with intense and cruel hate on St Stephen's Day.

(i) THE MAGPIE

There is no Irish name for the magpie. It is generally called *Francagh*, a Frenchman, though no one knows why. Many queer tales are narrated of this bird, arising from its quaint ways, its adroit cunning and habits of petty larceny. Its influence is not considered evil, though to meet one alone in the morning when going a journey is an ill omen, but to meet more than one magpie means good fortune, according to the old rhyme which runs thus:

One for Sorrow,
Two for Mirth,
Three for Marriage,
Four for a Birth.

(ii) THE WREN

The wren is mortally hated by the Irish – for on one occasion when the Irish troops were approaching to attack a portion of Cromwell's army, the wrens came and perched on the Irish drums and by their tapping and noise aroused the English soldiers, who fell on the Irish troops and killed them all. So ever since the Irish hunt the wren on St Stephen's Day and teach their children to run it through with thorns and kill it whenever it can be caught. A dead wren was also tied to a pole and carried from house to house by boys, who demanded money; if nothing was given the wren was buried on the door-step which was considered a great insult to the family and a degradation.

(iii) THE RAVEN AND WATER WAGTAIL

If ravens come cawing about a house it is a sure sign of death, for the raven is Satan's own bird. So also is the water wagtail, yet beware of killing it, for it has three drops of the devil's blood in its little body, and ill-luck always goes with it and follows it.

(iv) THE CUCKOO AND ROBIN REDBREAST

It is very unlucky to kill the cuckoo or break its eggs,

for it brings fine weather; but most unlucky of all things is to kill the robin redbreast. The robin is God's own bird, sacred and holy, and held in the greatest veneration because of the beautiful tradition current amongst the people that it was the robin plucked out the sharpest thorn that was piercing Christ's brow on the cross. In so doing the breast of the bird was dyed red with the Saviour's blood, and so has remained ever since a sacred and blessed sign to preserve the robin from harm and make it beloved of all men.

(v) THE CRICKET

The crickets are believed to be enchanted. People do not like to express an exact opinon about them, so they are spoken of with great mystery and awe and no one would venture to kill them for the whole world. But they are by no means evil, on the contrary, the presence of the cricket is considered lucky, and their singing keeps away the fairies at night, who are always anxious, in their selfish way, to have the whole hearth left clear for themselves that they may sit round the last embers of the fire and drink the cup of milk left for them by the farmer's wife, in peace and quietness. The crickets are supposed to be hundreds of years old and their talk, could we understand it, would no doubt be most interesting and instructive.

(vi) THE BEETLE

The beetle is not killed by the people for the following reason: they have a tradition that one day the chief priests sent messengers in every direction to look for the Lord Jesus and they came to a field where a man was reaping, and asked him:

'Did Jesus of Nazareth pass this way?'

'No,' said the man, 'I have not seen him.'

'But I know better,' said a little clock running up, 'for He was here today and rested, and has not long gone away.'

'That is false,' said a great big black beetle, coming forward. 'He has not passed since yesterday and you will never find Him on this road, try another.'

So the people kill the clock because he tried to betray Christ, but they spare the beetle and will not touch him because he saved the Lord on that day.

(vii) THE HARE

Hares are considered unlucky as the witches constantly assume their form in order to gain entrance to a field where they can bewitch the cattle. A man once fired at a hare he met in the early morning, and having wounded it, followed the track of the blood till it disappeared within a cabin. On entering he found Nancy Malony, the greatest witch in all the country, sitting by the fire, groaning and holding her side. And then the man knew that she had been out in the form of a hare and he rejoiced over her discomfort.

Still it is not lucky to kill a hare before sunrise, even when it crosses your path; but should it cross *three* times, then turn back, for danger is on the road before you.

A tailor one time returning home very late at night from a wake, or better, very early in the morning, saw a hare sitting on the path before him and it was not inclined to run away. As he approached, with his stick raised to strike her, he distinctly heard a voice saying, 'Don't kill it'. However, he struck the hare three times, and each time heard the voice say, 'Don't kill it'. But the last blow knocked the poor hare quite dead and immediately a great big weasel sat up and began to spit at him. This greatly frightened the tailor who, however, grabbed the hare and ran off as fast as he could. Seeing him look so pale and frightened, his wife asked the cause, and he told her the whole story. They both knew he had done wrong and offended some powerful witch, who would be avenged. However, they dug a grave for the hare and buried it for they were afraid to eat it and thought that now perhaps the danger was over. But next day the man became suddenly speechless and died off before the seventh day was over without a word evermore passing his lips. Then all the neighbours knew that the witch-woman had taken her revenge.

(viii) THE WEASEL

Weasels are spiteful and malignant, and old withered witches sometimes take this form. It is extremely unlucky to meet a weasel the first thing in the morning; still it would be hazardous to kill it for it might be a witch and take revenge. Indeed one should be very cautious about killing a weasel at any time, for all the other weasels will resent your audacity and kill your chickens when an opportunity offers. The only remedy is to kill one chicken yourself, make the sign of the cross solemnly three times over it, then tie it to a stick hung up in the yard and the weasels will have no more power for evil, nor the witches who take their form, at least during the year, if the stick is left standing, but the chicken may be eaten when the sun goes down.

(ix) CATS

The observation of cats is very remarkable and also their intense curiosity. They examine everything in a house and in a short time know all about it as well as the owner. They are never deceived by stuffed birds or any such weak human delusions. They fathom it all at one glance, and then turn away with apathetic indifference, as if saying, in cat language – 'We know all about it'.

A favourite cat in a gentleman's house was rather fond of nocturnal rambles and late hours, perhaps copying his master, but no matter what his engagements were the cat always returned regularly next morning precisely at nine o'clock, which was the breakfast hour, and *rang the house bell* at the hall door. This fact was stated to me on undoubted authority; and, in truth, there is nothing too wonderful to believe about the intellect of cats; no matter what strange things may be narrated of them, nothing should be held improbable or impossible to their intelligence.

But cats are decidely malific; they are selfish, revengeful, treacherous, cunning and generally dangerous. The evil spirit in them is easily aroused. It is a superstition that if you are going on a journey and meet a cat you should turn back. But the cat must meet you on the road, not simply be in the house; and it must look you full in the face. Then cross yourself and turn back; for a witch or a devil is in your path.

It is believed also that if a black cat is killed, and a bean placed in the heart, and the animal afterwards buried, the beans that grow from that seed will confer extraordinary power – for if a man places one in his mouth, he will become invisible and can go anywhere he likes without being seen.

The Irish have always looked on cats as evil and mysteriously connected with some demoniacal influence. On entering a house the usual salutation is: 'God save all here, except the cat.' Even the cake on the griddle may be blessed, but no one says, 'God bless the cat.'

It is believed that the devil often assumes the form of these animals. . . it is supposed that black cats have powers and faculties quite different from all other of the feline tribe. They are endowed with reason, can understand conversations and are quite able to talk if they considered it advisable and judicious to join in the conversation. Their temperament is exceedingly unamiable, they are artful, malignant and skilled in deception. People should be very cautious in caressing them for they have the venomous heart and the evil eye, and are ever ready to do an injury. Yet the liver of a black cat has the singular power to excite love when properly administered. If ground to powder and infused into potion, the recipient is fated to love passionately the person who offers it and has worked the charm.

Cats are revengeful, and one should be very careful not to offend them. A lady was in the habit of feeding the cat from her own table at dinner and no doubt giving it choice morsels, but one day there was a dinner party and pussy was quite forgotten. So she sulked and plotted revenge, and that night, after the lady was in bed, the cat, who had hidden herself in the room sprang at the throat of her friend and mistress and bit her so severely that in a week the lady died of virulent blood poisoning.

Yet it is singular that the blood of the black cat is esteemed of wonderful power, when mixed with herbs, for charms; and also of great efficacy in potions for the cure of disease; but three drops of the blood are sufficient, and it is generally obtained by nipping off a small piece of the tail.

(x) GENERAL SUPERSTITIONS

A goose is killed on St Michael's Day because the son of a king, being then at a feast, was choked by the bones of a goose; but was restored by St Patrick. Hence the king ordered a goose to be sacrificed every year on the anniversay of the day to commemorate the event and in honour of St Michael.

A fowl is killed on St Martin's Day and the blood sprinkled on the house. In Germany a black cock is substituted.

A crowing hen, a whistling girl and a black cat are considered most unlucky. Beware of them in a house.

If a cock comes on the threshold and crows you may expect visitors.

To see three magpies on the left hand when on a journey is unlucky – but two on the right hand is a good omen.

If you hear the cuckoo on your right hand you will have luck all the year after.

Whoever kills a robin redbreast will never have good

luck were they to live a thousand years.

A water wagtail near the house means bad news is on its way to you.

If the first lamb of the season is born black, it foretells mourning garments for the family within the year.

It is very lucky for a hen and her chickens to stray into your house.

It is good to meet a white lamb in the early morning with the sunlight on its face.

It is unlucky to meet a magpie, a cat, or a lame woman when going a journey. Or for a cock to meet a person in the doorway and crow before him – then the journey should be put off.

If one magpie comes chattering to your door it is a sign of death; but if two prosperity will follow. For a magpie to come to the door and look at you is a sure death-sign and nothing can avert the doom.

A flight of rooks over an army signals defeat; if over a house, or over people when driving or walking, death will follow.

It is very unlucky to ask a man on his way to fish where he is going. And many would turn back knowing that it was an evil spell.

When a swarm of bees suddenly quits the hive it is a sign that death is hovering near the house. But the evil may be averted by the powerful prayers and exorcism of the priest.

The shoe of a horse or of an ass nailed to the door-post will bring good luck; because these animals were in the stall when Christ was born and are blessed for evermore. But the shoe must be found, not given, in order to bring luck.

A hen that crows is very unlucky and should be killed; very often the hen is stoned for it is believed that she is bewitched by the fairies.

The cuttings of your hair should not be thrown where birds can find them; for they will take them to build their nests and then you will have headaches all the year after.

In whatever quarter you are looking when you first hear the cuckoo in the season, you will be travelling in that direction before the year is over.

It was the privilege of the chief bards to wear mantles made of birds' plumage. A short cape flung on the shoulders made of mallards' necks and crests must have been very gorgeous in effect, glittering like jewels, when the torch-light played on the colours at the festivals.

9 Marriage

In old times in Ireland it was thought right and proper to seem to use force in carrying off the bride to her husband. She was placed on a swift horse before the bridegroom, while all her kindred started in pursuit with shouts and cries. Twelve maidens attended the bride and each was placed on horseback behind the young men who rode after the bridal pair. On arriving at her future home, the bride was met on the threshold by the bridegroom's mother, who broke an oaten cake over her head as a good sign of plenty in the future. In the mountains where horses cannot travel, the bridal party walk in procession; the young men carrying torches of dried bogwood to light the bride over the ravines, for in winter the mountain streams are rapid and dangerous to cross.

The Celtic ceremonial of marriage resembles the ancient Greek ritual in many points. A traveller in Ireland some fifty years ago, before politics had quite killed romance and ancient tradition in the hearts of the people, thus describes a rustic marriage festival which he came on by chance one evening in the wilds of Kerry:

A large hawthorn tree that stood in the middle of a field near a stream was hung all over with bits of coloured stuff, while lighted rush candles were placed here and there amongst the branches to symbolise, no doubt, the new life of brightness preparing for the bridal pair. Then came a procession of boys marching slowly with flutes and pipes made of hollow reeds, and one struck a tin can with a stick at intervals, with a strong rhythmical sound. This represented the plectrum. Others rattled slates and bones between their fingers, and beat time, after the manner of the Crotolistrai – a rude attempt at music, which appears amongst all nations of the earth, even the most savage. A boy followed bearing a lighted torch of bogwood. Evidently he was Hymen and the flame of love was his cognisance. After him came the betrothed pair hand-in-hand, a large square canopy of black stuff being held over their heads – the emblem, of course, of the mystery of love, shrouded and veiled from the prying light of day.

Behind the pair followed two attendants bearing high over the heads of the young couple a sieve filled with meal – a sign of the plenty that would be in their house and an omen of good luck and the blessing of children.

A wild chorus of dancers and singers closed the procession; the chorus of the epithalamium, and grotesque figures, probably the traditional fauns and satyrs, nymphs and bacchanals, mingled together with mad laughter and shouts and waving of green branches.

The procession then moved on to a bonfire, evidently the ancient altar, and having gone round it three times the black shroud was lifted from the bridal pair and they kissed each other before all the people who shouted and waved their branches in approval.

Then the preparations for the marriage supper began, on which, however, the traveller left them, having laid some money on the altar as an offering of goodwill for the marriage future.

At the wedding supper there was always plenty of eating and drinking, and dancing and the feast were prolonged till near morning when the wedding song was sung by the whole party of friends standing while the bride and bridegroom remained seated at the head of the table. The chorus of one of these ancient songs may be thus literally translated from the Irish:

It is not day, nor yet day,
It is not day, nor yet morning;
It is not day, nor yet day,
For the moon is shining brightly.

Another marriage song was sung in Irish frequently, each verse ending with the lines:

There is a sweet enchanting music, and the
golden harps are ringing;
And twelve comely maidens deck the bride-bed
for the bride.

A beautiful new dress was presented to the bride by her husband at the marriage feast; at which also the father paid down her dowry before the assembled guests; and all the place round the house was lit by torches when night came on, and the song and the dance continued till daylight, with much speech-making and drinking of poteen.

All fighting was steadily avoided at a wedding; for a quarrel would be considered a most unlucky omen.

A wet day was also held to be very unlucky, as the

bride would assuredly weep for sorrow throughout the year. But the bright warm sunshine was hailed joyfully, according to the old saying

> Happy is the bride that the sun shines on;
> But blessed is the corpse that the rain rains on.

10   Herbs, Cures and Charms

The Irish, according to the saying of a wise man of
the race, are the last of the 305 great Celtic nations of
antiquity spoken of by Josephus, the Jewish historian.
They alone preserve inviolate the ancient venerable
language, minstrelsy and Bardic traditions, with the
strange and mystic secrets of herbs, through whose
potent powers they can cure disease, cause love or
hatred, discover the hidden mysteries of life and death
and dominate over the fairy wiles or the malific
demons.

The ancient people used to divine future events,
victory in wars, safety in a dangerous voyage, triumph
of a projected undertaking, success in love, recovery
from sickness or the approach of death – all through
the skilful use of herbs, the knowledge of which had
come down to them through the earliest traditions of
the human race. One of these herbs, called the Fairy-
plant, was celebrated for its potent power of divination; but only the experts knew the mystic manner of
its preparation for use.

There was another herb of which a drink was made,
called the Bardic potion, for the bards alone had the
secret of the herb and of the proper mode of treatment
by which its mystic power could be revealed. This
potion they gave their infant children at their birth,
for it had the singular property of endowing the recipient with a fairy sweetness of voice of the most raptur-
ous and thrilling charm. And instances are recorded

58

of men amongst the Celtic bards, who, having drunk of this potion in early life were ever after endowed with the sweet voice, like fairy music, that swayed the hearts of the hearers as they chose, to love or war, joy or sadness, as if by magic influence, or lulled them into the sweet calm of sleep. Such, according to the bardic legends, was the extraordinary powers of voice possessed by the great court minstrel of Fionn Ma-Coul, who resided with the great chief at his palace of Almhuin, and always sat next to him at the royal table.

The virtue of herbs is great, but they must be gathered at night, and laid in the hand of a dead man to hold. There are herbs that produce love and herbs that produce sterility; but only the fairy doctor knows the secrets of their power and he will reveal the knowledge to no man unless to an expert. The wise women learn the mystic powers from the fairies, but how they pay for the knowledge none dare to tell.

The fairy doctors are often seized with trembling while uttering a charm, and look round with a scared glance of terror as if some awful presence were beside them. But the people have the most perfect faith in the herb-men and wise women and the faith may often work the cure.

There are seven herbs of great value and power — they are ground ivy, vervain, eyebright, groundsel, foxglove, the bark of the elder tree and the young shoots of the hawthorn.

Nine balls of these mixed together may be taken and afterwards a potion made of bog-water and salt, boiled in a vessel, with a piece of money and an elf-stone.

The elf-stone is generally found near a rath; it has great virtues, but being once lifted up by the spade it must never again touch the earth or all its virtue is gone. This elf-stone is in reality only an ancient stone arrow-head.

The *Mead Cailleath*, or wood anemone, is used as a plaster for wounds.

The hazel tree has many virtues. It is sacred and powerful against devils' wiles and has mysteries and secret properties known to the wise and the experts. The ancient Irish believed that there were fountains at the head of the chief rivers of Ireland, over each of which grew nine hazel trees that at certain times produced beautiful red nuts. These nuts fell on the surface of the water and the salmon in the river came up and ate of them and this caused the red spots on the salmon. And whoever could catch and eat one of these salmon would be inbued with the sublimest poetic intellect. Hence the phrase current amongst the people: 'Had I the net of science', 'Had I eaten of the salmon of knowledge.' And this supernatural knowledge came to the great Fionn through the touch of a salmon and made him foreknow all events.

Of all the herbs the yarrow is the best for cures and potions. It is even sewn up in clothes as a preventive of disease.

The *Liss-more*, or great herb, has also strong healing

power, and is used as a charm.

There is a herb, also, or fairy grass, called the *Faud Shaughran*, or the 'stray sod', and whoever treads the path it grows on is compelled by an irresistible impulse to travel on without stopping, all through the night, delirious and restless, over bog and mountain, through hedges and ditches, till wearied and bruised and cut, his garments torn, his hands bleeding, he finds himself in the morning twenty or thirty miles, perhaps, from his own home. Those who fall under this strange influence have all the time the sensation of flying and are utterly unable to pause or turn back or change their career. There is, however, another herb that can neutralise the effects of the *Faud Shaughran*, but only the initiated can utilise its mystic properties.

Another grass is the *Fair-Gortha*, or the 'hunger-stricken sod', and if the hapless traveller accidentally treads on this grass by the road-side, while passing on a journey, either by night or day, he becomes at once seized with the most extraordinary cravings of hunger and weakness and unless timely relief is afforded he must certainly die.

When a child is sick a fairy woman is generally sent for and she makes a drink for the patient of those healing herbs of which she only has the knowledge. A childless woman is considered to have the strongest power over the secrets of herbs, especially those used for the maladies of children.

There is a herb, grown on one of the western islands off the coast of Connemara, which is reported to have great and mystic power. But no one will venture to pronounce its name. If it is desired to know for certain whether one lying sick will recover, the nearest relative must go out and look for the herb just as the sun is rising. And while holding it in the hand an ancient form of incantation must be said. If the herb remains fresh and green the patient will certainly recover; but if it wither in the hand while the words of the incantation are said over it, then the sick person is doomed. He will surely die.

It was from their great knowledge of the properties of herbs that the Tuatha-de-Dananns obtained the reputation of being sorcerers. At the great battle of Moytura in Mayo, fought about three thousand years ago, Dianecht, the great, wise Druid physician to the army, prepared a bath of herbs and plants in the line of the battle, of such wonderful curative power that the wounded who were plunged into it came out whole, it being a sovereign remedy for all diseases. But the king of the Tuatha having lost his hand in the combat, the bath had no power to heal him. So Dianecht made him a silver hand, and the monarch was ever after known in history as *Nuad Airgerat Lamh* (Nuad of the Silver Hand).

All herbs pulled on May Day Eve have a sacred healing power, if pulled in the name of the Holy Trinity; but if in the name of Satan, they work evil. Some herbs are malific if broken by the hand. So the plant is tied to a dog's foot, and when he runs it breaks, without a hand touching it and may be used with safety.

A man pulled a certain herb on May Eve to cure his son who was sick to death. The boy recovered, but disappeared and was never heard of after and the father died that day year. He had broken the fatal herb with the hand and so the doom fell on him.

Another man did the same, and gave the herb to his son to eat, who immediately began to bark like a dog, and so continued till he died.

The fatal herbs have signs known only to the fairy doctors, who should always be consulted before treating the sick in the family.

There are *seven* herbs that nothing natural or supernatural can injure; they are vervain, John's-wort, speedwell, eyebright, mallow, yarrow and self-help. But they must be pulled at noon on a bright day, near the full of the moon, to have full power.

It is firmly believed that the herb-women who perform cures receive their knowledge from the fairies, who impart to them the mystical secrets of herbs and where to find them; but these secrets must not be revealed except on the death-bed and then only to the eldest of the family.

Many mysterious rites are practised in the making and the giving of potions, and the messenger who carries the draught to the sufferer must never look behind him nor utter a word till he hands the medicine to the patient, who instantly swallows a cup of the mixture before other hands have touched it.

A celebrated doctor in the south was an old woman, who had lived seven years with the fairies. She performed wonderful cures and only required a silver tenpence to be laid on her table for the advice given and for the miraculous herb potion.

(i) A LOVE POTION

Some of the country people have still a traditional remembrance of very powerful herbal remedies and love potions are even now frequently in use. They are generally prepared by an old women; but must be administered by the person who wishes to inspire the tender passion. At the same time, to give a love potion is considered a very awful act as the result may be fatal or at least full of danger.

A fine, handsome young man, of the best character and conduct, suddenly became wild and reckless, drunken and disorderly, from the effect, it was believed, of a love potion administered to him by a young girl who was passionately in love with him. When she saw the change produced in him by her act, she became moody and nervous, as if a constant terror were over her, and no one ever saw her smile again. Finally, she became half deranged and after a few years of a strange, solitary life, she died of melancholy and despair. This was said to be 'The Love-potion Curse.'

(ii) LOVE DREAMS

The girl who wishes to see her future husband must go out and gather certain herbs in the light of the full moon of the new year, repeating this charm:

Moon, moon , tell unto me
When my true love I shall see?
What fine clothes am I to wear?
How many children shall I bear?
For if my love comes not to me
Dark and dismal my life will be.

Then the girl, cutting three pieces of clay from the sod with a black-hafted knife, carries them home, ties them up in the left stocking with the right garter, places the parcel under her pillow, and dreams a true dream of the man she is to marry and of all her future fate.

(iii) TO CAUSE LOVE

Ten leaves of the hemlock dried and powdered and mixed in food or drink will make the person you like to love you in return. Also keep a sprig of mint in your hand till the herb grows moist and warm, then take hold of the hand of the woman you love, and she will follow you as long as the two hands close over the herb. No invocation is necessary; but silence must be kept between the two parties for ten minutes, to give the charm time to work with due success.

(A Wicked Spell)

When a girl wishes to gain the love of a man, and to make him marry her, the dreadful spell is used called *Drimial Agus Thorial.* At dead of night, she and an accomplice go to a churchyard, exhume a newly-buried corpse and take a strip of the skin from the head to the heel. This is wound round the girl as a belt with a solemn invocation to the devil for his help.

After she has worn it for a day and a night she watches her opportunity and ties it round the sleeping man whose love she desires; during which process the name of God must not be mentioned.

When he awakes the man is bound by the spell and is forced to marry the cruel and evil harpy. It is said the children of such marriages bear a black mark round the wrist, and are known and shunned by the people, who call them 'sons of the devil'.

(iv) GENERAL CURES

It is said by the wise women and fairy doctors that the roots of the elder tree, and the roots of an apple tree that bears red apples, if boiled together and drunk fasting, will expel any evil living thing or evil spirit that may have taken up its abode in the body of a man.

But an evil charm to produce a living thing in the body can also be made, by pronouncing a certain magic and wicked spell over the food or drink taken by any person that an enemy wishes to injure.

One should therefore be very cautious in accepting anything to eat from a person of known malicious tongue and spiteful heart, or who has an ill will against you, for poison lies in their glance and in the touch of their hands; and an evil spell is in their very presence, and on all they do, say, or touch.

A bunch of mint tied round the wrist is a sure remedy for disorders of the stomach.

Nettles gathered in a churchyard and boiled down for a drink have the power to cure dropsy.

An iron ring worn on the fourth finger was considered effective against rheumatism by the Irish peasantry from ancient times.

Paralysis is cured by stroking, but many forms and mystic incantations are also used during the process; and only certain persons have the power in the hands that can effect a cure by the magic of the stroke.

The seed of docks tied to the left arm of a woman will prevent her being barren.

A spoonful of *aqua vitae* sweetened with sugar, and a little grated bread added so that it may not annoy the brain or the liver, will preserve from lethargy and apoplexy and all cold diseases.

The juice of carrots boiled down is admirable for purifying the blood.

Clippings of the hair and nails of a child tied up in a linen cloth and placed under the cradle will cure convulsions.

To cure fever, place the patient on the sandy shore when the tide is coming in, and the retreating waves will carry away the disease and leave him well.

Tober Maire (Mary's well), near Dundalk, has a great reputation for cures. Thousands used to visit it on Lady Day for weak eyesight and the lowness of heart. Nine times they must go round the well on their knees, always westward. Then drink a cup of the water, and not only are they cured of their ailment but are as free from sin as the angels in heaven.

(v) FOR PAINS IN THE BODY

Rub the part affected with flax and tow, heated in the fire, repeating in Irish:

'In the name of a rough man and a mild woman, and of the Lamb of God, be healed from your pains and your sins. So be it. Amen.'

This custom refers to the tradition that one day the Lord Christ, being weary, asked leave to rest in a house, but was refused by the master of the house, a rough, rude man. Then the wife, being a mild woman, had pity on the wayfarer and brought Him in to rest, gave Him a cup of water to drink and spoke kindly to Him. The man was suddenly taken with severe pains and seemed likely to die in his agony.

On this Christ called for some flax and tow, and, breathing on it, placed it on the part affected and the man was quite healed. Then the Lord Christ went His way, but not before the man had humbly asked pardon for his rudeness to a stranger.

The tradition of this cure has remained ever since, and a hot plaster of flax and tow is used by the peasantry invariably for all sudden pains, and found to be most successful as a cure.

(vi) FOR TOOTHACHE

Go to a graveyard; kneel upon any grave; say three paters and three aves for the soul of the dead lying beneath. Then take a handful of grass from the grave, chew it well, casting forth each bite without swallowing any portion. After this process the sufferer, were he to live a hundred years, will never have toothache any more.

Another

The patient must vow a vow to God, the Virgin and the new moon, never to comb his hair on a Friday, in remembrance of relief should he be cured; and whenever or wherever he first sees the moon he must fall on his knees and say five prayers in gratitude for the cure, even if crossing a river at the time.

Another

Carry in your pocket the two jaw-bones of a haddock; for ever since the miracle of the loaves and fishes these bones are an infallible remedy against toothache, and the older they are the better, as they are nearer the time of the miracle.

Also this charm is to be sewn on the clothes:

> As Peter sat on a marble stone,
> The Lord came to him all alone,
> 'Peter, Peter, what makes you shake?'
> 'O Lord and Master, it is the toothache.'
> Then Christ said, 'Take these for My sake,
> And never more you'll have toothache.'

To avoid toothache never shave on a Sunday.

(vii) FOR FRECKLES

Anoint a freckled face with the blood of a bull, or of a hare, and it will put away the freckles and make the skin fair and clear. Also the distilled water of walnuts is good.

(viii) FOR A BURN

There is a pretty secret to cure a burn without a scar: Take a sheep's suet and the rind of the elder tree, boil both together, and the ointment will cure a burn without leaving a mark.

(ix) FOR THE MEMORY

The whitest of frankincense beaten fine and drunk in white wine, wonderfully assists the memory, and is profitable for the stomach also.

(x) FOR THE FALLING SICKNESS

Take a hank of grey yarn, a lock of the patient's hair, some parings of his nails and bury them deep in the earth, repeating in Irish, as a burial service, 'Let the great sickness lie there for ever. By the power of Mary and the soul of Paul, let the great sickness lie buried in the clay, and never more rise out of the ground. AMEN.'

If the patient, on awaking from sleep, calls out the name of the person who uttered these words, his recovery is certain.

If a person crosses over the patient while he is in a

fit, or stands between him and the fire, then the sickness will stick to him and depart from the other that was afflicted.

(xi) FOR CHIN-COUGH

A griddle cake made of meal, to be given, not bought or made; but a cake *given* of love or of charity, not for begging; a cake given freely, with a prayer and a blessing; and from the breakfast of a man and his wife who had the same name before marriage – this is the cure.

The touch of a piebald horse. Even a piebald horse pawing before the door helps the cure.

The child to be passed seven times under and over an ass while a red string is tied on the throat of the patient.

Nine hairs from the tail of a black cat, chopped up and soaked in water, which is then swallowed, and the cough will be relieved.

(xii) FOR RHEUMATISM

The operator makes passes, like the mesmerist, over the member affected by the rheumatic pain, never touching the part, but moving his hand slowly over it at some distance, while he mutters a form of words in a low voice.

(xiii) FOR A STYE ON THE EYELID

Point a gooseberry thorn at it nine times, saying, 'Away, away, away!' and the stye will vanish presently and disappear.

(xiv) TO CURE WARTS

On meeting a funeral, take some of the clay from under the feet of the men who bear the coffin and apply it to the wart, wishing strongly at the same time that it may disappear, and so it will be.

(xv) FOR A STITCH IN THE SIDE

Rub the part affected with unsalted butter and make the sign of the cross seven times over the place.

(xvi) FOR WEAK EYES

A decoction of the flowers of daisies boiled down is an excellent wash, to be used constantly.

(xvii) FOR WATER ON THE BRAIN

Cover the head well with wool, then place oil-skin over it, and the water will be drawn up out of the head. When the wool is quite saturated the brain will be free and the child cured.

(xviii) FOR HIP DISEASE

Take three green stones, gathered from a running brook, between midnight and morning, while no word is said. In silence it must be done. Then uncover the limb and rub each stone several times closely downwards from the hip to the toe, saying in Irish:

Wear away, wear away,
There you shall not stay,
Cruel pain – away, away.

(xix) FOR THE MUMPS

Wrap the child in a blanket, take it to the pigsty, rub the child's head to the back of a pig, and the mumps will leave it and pass from the child to the animal.

Another
Take nine black stones, gathered before sunrise and

bring the patient with a rope round his neck to a holy well – not speaking all the while. Then cast in three stones in the name of God, three in the name of Christ and three in the name of Mary. Repeat this process for three mornings and the disease will be cured.

(xx) FOR EPILEPSY

Take nine pieces of young elder twig, run a thread of silk of three strands through the pieces, each piece being an inch long. Tie this round the patient's neck next to the skin. Should the thread break and the amulet fall, it must be buried deep in the earth and another amulet made like the first, for if once it touches the ground the charm is lost.

Another

Take nine pieces of a dead man's skull, grind them to powder and then mix with a decoction of wall rue. Give the patient a spoonful of this mixture every morning fasting, till the whole potion is swallowed. None must be left or the dead man would come to look for the pieces of his skull.

(xxi) FOR DEPRESSION OF THE HEART

When a person becomes low and depressed and careless about everything, as if all vital strength and energy had gone, he is said to have got a fairy blast. And blast-water must be poured over him by the hands of a fairy doctor while saying, 'In the name of the saint with the sword, who has strength before God and stands at His right hand.' Great care must be taken that no portion of water is profaned. Whatever is left after the operation must be poured on the fire.

(xxii) FOR THE FAIRY DART

Fairy darts are generally aimed at the fingers, causing the joints to swell and grow red and inflamed. An eminent fairy-woman made the cure of fairy darts her speciality. She was sent for by all the country round and was generally successful. But she had no power unless *asked* to make the cure and she took no reward at the time, not till the patient was cured and the dart extracted. The treatment included a great many prayers and much anointing with a salve of which she only had the secret. Then she proceeded to extract the dart with great solemnity, working with a small instrument, on the point of which she finally produced the dart. This proved to be a bit of flax artfully laid under the skin by the malicious fairies causing all the evil, and of course on seeing the flax no one could doubt the power of the operator and the grateful patient paid his fee.

(xxiii) A CURE FOR CATTLE

Take nine leaves of the male crowfoot, plucked on a Sunday night: bruise them on a stone that never was moved since the world began, and never can be moved. Mix with salt and spittle, and apply the plaster to the ear of the sick beast. Repeat this three times for a man, and twice for a horse.

(xxiv) A CHARM FOR SAFETY

Pluck ten blades of yarrow, keep nine, and cast the tenth away for tithe to the spirits. Put the nine in your stocking, under the heel of the right foot when going a journey, and the Evil One will have no power over you.

(xxv) A CHARM FOR THE FAIRY-STROKE

There is a very ancient and potent charm which may be tried with great effect in case of a suspected fairy-stroke.

Place three rows of salt on a table in three lines, three equal measures to each row. The person performing the spell then encloses the rows of salt with his arm, leaning his head down over them, while he repeats the Lord's Prayer three times over each row –

that is nine times in all. Then he takes the hand of the one who has been fairy-struck and says over it, 'By the power of the Father, and of the Son, and of the Holy Spirit, let this disease depart, and the spell of the evil spirits be broken! I adjure, I command you to leave this man [naming him]. In the name of God I pray; in the name of Christ I adjure; in the name of the Spirit of God I command and compel you to go back and leave this man free! AMEN! AMEN! AMEN!'

(xxvi) TO FIND STOLEN GOODS

Place two keys on a sieve, in the form of a cross. Two men hold the sieve, while a third makes the sign of the cross on the forehead of the suspected party, and calls out his name loudly, three times over. If innocent, the keys remain stationary; but if guilty, the keys revolve slowly round the sieve and then there is no doubt as to who is the thief.

(xxvii) HOW TO HAVE MONEY ALWAYS

Kill a black cock and go to the meeting of three crossroads where a murderer is buried. Throw the dead bird over your left shoulder then and there, after nightfall, in the name of the devil, holding a piece of money in your hand all the while. And ever after, no matter what you spend, you will always find the same piece of money undiminished in your pocket.

11 Dreams

Never tell your dreams fasting, and always tell them first to a woman called Mary.

To dream of a hearse with white plumes is a wedding; but to dream of a wedding is grief, and death will follow.

To dream of a woman kissing you is deceit; but of a man, friendship; and to dream of a horse exceedingly lucky.

To dream of a priest is bad; even to dream of the devil is better. Remember, also, either a present or a purchase from a priest is unlucky.

12 Omens and Superstitions

Auguries and prophecies of coming fate may also be obtained from the flight of birds, the motion of the winds, from sneezing, dreams, and the signs from a verse of the Psalter or Gospels. The peasantry attach great importance to the first verses of St John's Gospel and maintain that when the cock crows in the morning he is repeating these verses, from the first to the fourteenth, and if we understood the language of animals and birds, we could often hear them quoting these same verses.

A charm against sickness is an amulet worn round the neck, enclosing a piece of paper, on which is written the first three verses of St John's Gospel.

Omens that forbode evil
To stick a penknife in the mast of a boat when sailing is most unlucky.

To meet a man with red hair, or a woman with a red petticoat, the first thing in the morning.

To kill the robin redbreast.

To pass a churn and not give a helping hand.

To meet a funeral and not go back three steps with it.

To have a hare cross your path before sunrise.

To take away a lighted sod on May days or churning days, for fire is the most sacred of all things and you take away the blessing from the house along with it.

* * *

The Irish are very susceptible to omens. They say, 'Beware of a childless woman who looks fixedly at your child.'

Fire is the holiest of all things. Walk three times round a fire on St John's Eve and you will be safe from disease for all that year.

It is particularly unlucky to meet a red-haired man the first thing in the morning. There is a tradition that Judas Iscariot had red hair and it is from this the superstitious dread of the evil interference of a red-haired man may have orginated.

Never begin work on a Friday.

Never remove from a house or leave a situation on Saturday.

Never begin to make a dress on Saturday, or the wearer will die within the year.

Never mend a tear in a dress while it is on you, or

evil and malicious reports will be spread about you.

To throw a slipper after a party going a journey is lucky. Also to breakfast by candle-light on Christmas morning.

It is fatal at a marriage to tie a knot in a red handkerchief and only an enemy would do it. To break the spell the handkerchief should be burned.

The first days of the year and of the week are the luckiest. Never begin a journey on a Friday or Saturday, nor move from your residence, nor change a situation. Never cut out a dress or begin to make it on a Friday, nor fix a marriage, for of all days the fairies have the most malific power on a Friday. They are present then, and hear all that is said, therefore beware of speaking ill of them for they will work some evil if offended.

Never pay away money on the first Monday of the year, or you will lose your luck in gaining money all the year after.

Presents may be given on New Year's Day, but no money should be paid away.

Those who marry in autumn will die in spring.

The yew tree, the ash and the elder tree were sacred. The willow has a mystery in it of sound. The harp of King Brian Boru was made of willow wood.

When a servant leaves her place, if her mistress gives her a piece of bread let her put by some of it carefully, for as long as she has it good luck will follow her.

If a chair falls as a person rises, it is an unlucky omen.

It is unlucky to meet a cat, a dog, or a woman, when going out first in the morning; but unlucky above all is it to meet a woman with red hair the first thing in the morning when going on a journey, for her presence brings ill-luck and certain evil.

It is unlucky to pass under a hempen rope; the person who does so will die a violent death, or is fated to commit an evil act in after life, so it is decreed.

Do not put out a light while people are at supper, or there will be one less at the table before the year is out.

Never give any salt or fire while churning is going on. To upset the salt is exceedingly unlucky and a bad omen; to avert evil gather up the salt and fling it over the right shoulder into the fire, with the left hand.

The fortunate possessor of the four-leaved shamrock will have luck in gambling, luck in racing, and witchcraft will have no power over him. But he must always carry it about his person, and never give it away, or even show it to another.

A purse made from a weasel's skin will never want for money; but the purse must be found, not given or made.

If a man is ploughing, no one should cross the path of the horses.

It is unlucky to steal a plough, or take anything by stealth from a smith's forge.

When yawning make the sign of the cross instantly over the mouth, or the evil spirit will make a rush down and take up his abode within you.

Never give away water before breakfast, nor milk while churning is going on.

A married woman should not walk upon graves or her child will have a club-foot. If by accident she treads on a grave she must instantly kneel down, say a prayer, and make the sign of the cross on the sole of her shoe three times over.

Never take an infant in your arms, nor turn your head to look at it without saying, 'God bless it'. This keeps away the fatal influence of the Evil Eye.

It is asserted that on Christmas morning the ass

kneels down in adoration of Christ, and if a person can manage to touch the cross on the back of the animal at that particular moment the wish of his heart will be granted, whatever it may be.

When taking possession of a new house, every one should bring in some present, however trifling, but nothing should be taken away, and a prayer should be said in each corner of your bedroom, and some article of your clothing be deposited there at the same time.

If by accident, you find the back tooth of a horse, carry it about with you as long as you live and you will never want money; but it must be found by chance.

When a family has been carried off by fever, the house where they died may be again inhabited with safety if a certain number of sheep are driven in to sleep there for three nights.

If pursued at night by an evil spirit, or the ghost of one dead, and you hear footsteps behind you, try and reach a stream of running water, for if you can cross it, no devil or ghost will be able to follow you.

There are many superstitions prevalent in the Western Islands which are implicitly believed and acted on. Fishermen when going to sea must always enter the boat by the right side, no matter how inconvenient.

A coal of fire thrown after the fisherman brings him

good fortune.

A sick person must not be visited on a Friday, nor by any person who has just quitted a wake and looked upon the dead. The hair and nails of a sick person must not be cut till after recovery.

A whitethorn stick is a very unlucky companion on a journey; but a hazel switch brings good luck and has power over the devil.

If you want a person to win at cards, stick a crooked pin in his coat.

The ancient arrowheads, called elf-stones by the people, are used as charms to guard the cattle.

It is not safe to take an unbaptised child in your arms without making the sign of the cross over it.

It is unlucky to give a coal of fire out of the house before the child is baptised. And a piece of iron should be sewn in the infant's clothes and kept there till after the baptism.

Take a piece of bride-cake and pass it three times through a wedding-ring, then sleep on it, and you will see in a dream the face of your future spouse.

It is unlucky to accept a lock of hair, or a four-footed beast from a lover.

To make the skin beautiful, wash the face in May dew upon May morning just at sunrise.

If the palm of your hand itches you will be getting money, if the elbow, you will be changing beds; if the ear itches and is red and hot, some one is speaking ill of you.

If three drops of water are given to an infant before it is baptised, it will answer the first three questions put to it.

The seventh son of a seventh son has power over all diseases, and can cure them by laying on of hands; and a son born after his father's death has power over fevers.

MORE MERCIER BESTSELLERS

SUPERSTITIONS OF THE IRISH COUNTRY PEOPLE
Padraic O'Farrell

Living in its fullest sense is still dear to the Irish country folk and is reflected in their customs. Going to work, to sea, to weddings or wakes – at all of these there are fascinating customs to be observed.

FOLKTALES OF THE IRISH COUNTRYSIDE
Kevin Danaher

A delightful collection of stories of giants, of ghosts, of wondrous deeds, queer happenings, of fairies and the great kings of Ireland who had beautiful daughters and many problems.

GEMS OF IRISH WISDOM
Irish Proverbs and Sayings
Padraic O'Farrell

This book is full of the gems of Irish colloquial wit and wisdom. 'There is more wisdom spat into the *griosach* than you'd pick up in a year's book learning.'

A HISTORY OF IRISH FAIRIES
Carolyn White

In *A History of Irish Fairies* we find all the magic of the 'wee people'. The author deals with their important place in country folklore and tells us of their mannerisms, clothing, food and love-life.

www.ingramcontent.com/pod-product-compliance
Lightning Source LLC
Chambersburg PA
CBHW031447280326
41927CB00037B/387